WHAT DIFFERENCE
DOES IT MAKE?

WHAT DIFFERENCE DOES IT MAKE?

The Busy Person's Guide to Christianity

J. Brooke-Harte

ELM HILL

A Division of
HarperCollins Christian Publishing

www.elmhillbooks.com

What Difference Does It Make?

The Busy Person's Guide to Christianity

Published in Nashville, Tennessee, by Elm Hill, an imprint of Thomas Nelson. Elm Hill and Thomas Nelson are registered trademarks of HarperCollins Christian Publishing, Inc.

Elm Hill titles may be purchased in bulk for educational, business, fund-raising, or sales promotional use. For information, please e-mail SpecialMarkets@ThomasNelson.com.

Library of Congress Cataloging-in-Publication Data

Library of Congress Control Number: 2019906045

ISBN 978-1-400325740 (Paperback)
ISBN 978-1-400325757 (eBook)

DEDICATION

This book is dedicated to Dr. F. Brooks Sanders
—my father, my teacher, my friend.
There was never a question I had, never a problem too great
or too small, but that you would listen and answer it.
I remember fondly our times of batting around theological
ideas. We challenged each other a lot. Then you would go to
the Hebrew or Greek to examine all the options until the
answer was found.
Now you've gone on ahead, but someday I'll catch up in that
place where all questions will finally be answered, and we'll
bask in the greatness of our God.

Thanks Dad. I love you.

CONTENTS

INTRODUCTION

Why do some people think Christianity is the only path to God? How do we know it's true? Is it any different or better than other religions? Do absolutes exist?

Have those questions ever crossed your mind?

Possibly, this short book will spark a flame of new ideas regarding what God intends to be *for* you, in you, and through you.

Both believers and unbelievers carry many different ideas about what it means to be a Christian. As a believer, I hope you glean some new thoughts from mine.

J. Brooke-Harte

CHAPTER ONE

WHERE ARE WE AND WHERE ARE WE GOING?

WHERE ARE WE AND WHERE ARE WE GOING?

"You've just grown up that way. That's the only reason you believe it," Larry chimed in while the conversation ventured into uncharted waters that made him uncomfortable.

As the Marketing Director of a mall, I was at lunch with one of the media sales guys and I'd dared to bring up the forbidden subject of faith.

He was a six-foot, three-inch, two-hundred-twenty-pound, blonde-haired, blue-eyed hunk of Vietnam veteran. He'd seen it all, done it all, been scarred by it all, and was the ultimate tough guy.

His reaction was not uncommon, though. I'd heard it before, but I didn't think it was true.

Sure, I'd studied more than most since my father was a minister, a philosopher, and a professor. Plus, I'd had an advantage of learning from some of the greatest theologians in the country. But that was beside the point. For me, it was a heart thing.

"Well Larry," I continued. "What would it take for you to believe that what I'm telling you is true?"

"If I saw Him," he answered without a blink.

"You're a tough one!" I responded with a smile. "He's got your number, though, whether you believe it or not. And He loves you too."

With that, the subject got changed and we finished our coffee.

When I got into my car to return to the office, I said to the Lord, "Well, You heard it. I know You don't make many guest appearances these days, but if You wouldn't mind…"

About three weeks later, Larry and I had lunch again. This is the story he told.

"I had an interesting experience after that last time we met," he began.

"Yeah? What happened?" I said.

"Well, about a week after that lunch, I went to sleep and experienced something that was more real and different than any dream I've ever had. In fact, I don't think it was even exactly a dream."

"All of a sudden I was in this big, open, dark place that was sort of like the inside of a huge airplane hangar. Then I saw an almost blinding beam of light coming toward me. It was overpowering. I went down on my knees. *No one could stand in that presence. It's not possible.*"

I couldn't believe this was coming from Larry.

"You did it, Lord. You really did it!" I thought to myself. I silently cheered. I couldn't believe Larry admitted (humbly too) that *no one* could stand in *His* presence. Was the tough guy admitting that someone was tougher than he was?

He went on, "The light kept coming toward me and I've never felt so much love in my life. I never wanted that feeling to leave. Then He took me away on sort of a...I guess you would call it *a tour*. He showed me a lot of different things. Basically, let's just say He was showing me options. Then, we were back in the hangar.

"My wife was trying to wake me up because I was gasping and crying out. She thought I must be having a nightmare. But nothing fazed me."

"Finally, I was back in my bed sweating like a pig. It's an experience I'll never forget."

"Okay, you're right. *He's real*," he admitted with a degree of both reverence and chagrin in his voice.

I'd had my own experiences with the presence of God. I knew God was real. But at that early stage of life, how many occasions had I actually had to prove it? Some...but not a lot.

I had to admit that I'd done a lot more book learning than practical learning. Some of my theological ideas had been assumed in a kind of religious osmosis. A few of them had been put into the personal test tube of life, though, and found to be true.

Ultimately, however, my belief system and everyone's belief system are formed and validated where reality kicks us in the seat, and the truth of what we believe rises to the occasion or turns us in a different direction.

So, I ask you: Does each of us create his own faith? Is it based on emotions? Is it self-generated? Is it simply a family heirloom? Is faith mostly a figment of our imaginations or of someone else's? Does it actually make any difference? Isn't it a crutch? Aren't all religions pretty much the same with different window dressings? How do you find the "truth?" Doesn't everyone have to find his own truth? Are there absolutes? *Doesn't our total understanding of life and how we live it come down to what is true and what is truth?* If we're honest, all of these are questions we've probably asked ourselves at one point or another. They're ones for which I hope to offer some answers or at least give some food for thought. But the most important question...the critical question, *is finding truth.* Truth, by its very definition, is universal. It's something that's reliable, right, trustworthy, sure, faithful, and verifiable.

The comment that people often make in today's world is, "Well, what's true for one person may not be true for another." That reasoning can be used, of course, in relative statements like, "My mother is a great pianist." That's true for her...not for me. I'm a mother and I'm not a great pianist. Because my mother is a great pianist, we cannot draw the conclusion, therefore, that every mother is a great pianist or any other such extrapolations. The statement is therefore true, without rising to the premise of being *truth*.

I remember one year, a bunch of kids from church went off to summer camp and told this unsuspecting guy who'd never played ping-pong that you got two points for hitting the ball *under* the net. They told him a bunch of other crazy rules that were totally bogus too. But he didn't know until he actually started to play that he'd been scammed. Playing by those rules, he was doomed. He could never win. His ping-pong game would always remain "a mess."

If whatever we believe isn't the truth, the results are not going to be good however much we might enjoy the delusions of the moment. If claims and results don't correlate with suppositions, either some information is wrong or some information is missing. And our game of life will always remain "a mess."

So, how do you validate truth?

Scientifically, we validate from studying data, making observations, and drawing conclusions. Philosophically, it's the same. We validate truth through individual and collective observation, correlation of experience, historical data, clear reasoning, and substantiation of that which has been proposed or witnessed.

So, let's do some studying and observing. Let's begin by looking at where we are as a culture. Let's consider how we're doing on this planet called Earth.

If I had to describe our world in a word, it would be "stressed." I heard a great definition of that word a while back—it was *"Stress is the difference between expectation and reality."*

Even when it comes to small things, like expecting a phone call, if you wait and it doesn't come, it's stress. What I'm waiting for could be with great anticipation, thereby producing positive stress; or it might be with dread, producing negative stress. But either one is stress in the waiting, whether for good or bad.

Think about it. Everything that stresses us has to do with some state of limbo or lack of control in one way or another. Any form of the unknown opens the door to stress.

Haven't we all heard people say, "I'd rather just know! It's this not knowing that's killing me!"

<u>*What we expect or hope for vs. reality = stress.*</u>
Stress is, in fact, a form of fear.
And <u>fear is always of something in the future.</u>
Fear lives in the future tense.

. . . .

My father shared this concept with me many years ago. I've tested it and he was absolutely right. Even in the worst thing I've ever experienced, I can cope with it in the moment.

It's thoughts like *I wonder if this is going to get worse? Or how much longer can I stand this? Or is there something else I can do that I haven't already thought of? Or, will this ever change?* that get me. Always, it has to do with the future, even if just a second into the future....

I'm reminded of a story that was told to me by a missionary friend of mine, Hermano Pablo. He ministered in South America. Once when he was traveling with his young family down some of the back mountain roads, a torrential rain stopped them in their tracks. The road turned into mucky peanut butter and soon they were mired up to the floor boards. They were thoroughly stuck in the mud!

It was pouring, hot, and muggy. This was before the days of air-conditioning too, so if they put the windows down, they would get drenched. And if they left them up, they would get sweltered. Hermano Pablo made his best attempt to unstick them, spinning the wheels forward and then backward. But it only set them deeper in the mud. Finally he gave up and just sat there waiting for the rain to stop.

"Are we gonna be here forever, Dad?" came the disgruntled plea from his five-year-old son in the back seat.

Solemnly, he replied, "Yes, son, we're going to be here forever."

"No we're not, Dad!" returned the little voice with an unmistakable "Now you're kidding me" confident smile in it. Precious. The son knew his father. And he knew his father would not let them stay there forever.

This was not an indefinite eternal circumstance. It seemed so real as they sat there, and so silly when it was finally voiced. But the fear was obvious and the impatience palpable. To be sure, it wasn't all that comfortable in the car! But they were *okay*. They had comfortable seating. The pelting of the rain made a sort of pleasant sound and gave a fresh smell to the air. They had each other for entertainment and comfort. They weren't starving. No wild animals were attacking. Yes … at the moment, they were all right.

Living in the present moment, they were safe and protected. Their reality was just different from their expectation or desires.

Fear, in all of its trauma, is merely an illusion, a shadow, a *future* foreboding planted in our hearts from the adversary. Almost everything we fear never happens. And on the few occasions that it does, God is in the process of turning it for our good and proving his faithfulness. Even when we ignore His efforts, He continues to give us more chances. A new choice or a new opportunity will always emerge.

Jehovah God refers to Himself simply as "I AM" (Exodus 3:14). Seems like sort of a strange name, doesn't it? But He's actually telling us that *He's complete present tense, and He's present tense in everything that is.*

The time continuum is something created for our world. But with Him, everything is present tense. When we get to the future, He will be there because, then, it will be our present.

More than any other biblical instruction, the one most often given is "Fear not." But instructions or otherwise, the truth is that we live in a world of fear, anger, and isolation. Despite all admonitions and all of our sophistication, education, and communication tools, we still regularly hit that limbo space between expectation and reality.

Does it bother you that we need metal detectors in our schools? Is it disconcerting to watch the disrespect and conflict in homes, churches, and communities? Do you have trouble with the pounding negative barrage from the news media? Is it disheartening to be exposed to the stress, lostness, rage, and dysfunction running rampant in our neighborhoods and in our world?

What do we do with the words of Jesus—"Peace I leave with you, my peace I give unto you; not as the world gives, give I unto you. Let not your heart be troubled, neither let it be afraid" (John 14:27, KJV). These words may seem impossible, however relevant.

How about when He said, "Strait is the gate, and narrow is the way which leadeth unto life, and few there be that find it" (Matthew 7:14). Why is that? Is this some kind of game? And what is this *life* He's talking about?

Sometimes, words fail us. Sometimes, our English language is vague. For example, our English word for *life* is all-encompassing. But in the original script of the New Testament, the Greek word for life is specific. In Greek (and Aramaic—the two original languages of the New Testament, and Hebrew—the original language of the Old Testament), words are more descriptive.

Hebrew, for example, is a picture-painting language. In the vernacular, instead of saying "He's strong," they might say, "He's like a rock." On the other hand, the Greek might say something more descriptive like "He's a mighty man of valor." Our quick, flat English version is often less specific. At any rate, the word "life," in this case, comes from the Greek word *"Zoë." Zoë means vitality. It means life as God knows it—the very life of God in us.*

Specifically, it's not another Greek word for life— "bios." *Bios refers to daily existence, our present state of being, our occupational life.* Bios is on the outside. Zoë is on the inside. It's the internal life that Jesus is talking about. The delineation is specific in the original language.

I think the Lord says there are few who find it because He knows how easy it is for us to get distracted, self-absorbed, and caught up in lies and distortions. He knows how easy it is for us to just become survivors, hanging on for dear life, trying to ride the waves of our bios, and not even taking time to discover all that He intends for us to have or to be in His Zoë.

He says specifically, "I am come that they might have life (Zoë) and that they might have it more abundantly" (John 10:10, KJV). And that's a standing offer. If you take that verse with a degree of skepticism, it may be because you haven't seen a lot of abundant lives. Or, perhaps, your own life is in that category.

Could it be that the offer has never really been accepted, or that it's a judgment based on bios? In that case, the promise doesn't apply. In fact, He promises that *we will* experience difficulties in our daily (bios) lives. It's His Spirit that He came to give us abundantly. It's the inside thing, the new heart, the new attitude, the new perspective.

It's important that we're sure we mean the same

thing by the words we use, though. I heard Ken Ham, an Australian, tell the story of coming to the U.S. and having battery trouble with his car. He took it to the mechanic and said, "My battery's flat." To which the mechanic replied, "What'd you do, run over it? You mean it's dead?" To which Ken replied, "No, it's not dead. It never was alive."

Another time, much to his embarrassment, he asked the babysitter if she'd like to nurse the baby. After getting a shocked and horrified look, he realized she was offended, so he said, "Okay then, I'll nurse it." (In Australia, to nurse a baby means to hold the baby.) Hmmm … words we think we know sometimes mean different things to different people.

So, as we progress, we're going to look at some terms and words which might not be totally clear to all. Misunderstood terms result in confused belief systems. And there are a lot of terms and belief systems out there. Everything people do is colored by their world view. Everything is seen through the glasses of conviction. So, let's take a brief look at some of the most popular belief systems, and some terms too.

Something to Think About:

How would you describe *your* world today?

What part does fear play in your life?

How much of what you fear ever happens?

Have you ever experienced a "God moment" in your life? Was there a time when you could see that God was directly involved?

What's the difference between Zoë life and bios life?

What role of God talked about in this chapter impacted you?

Who is ultimately responsible for what you think and what you believe?

CHAPTER TWO

COMPARATIVE GLIMPSES
AS A STARTING POINT...

COMPARATIVE GLIMPSES
AS A STARTING POINT...

When I was a junior in high school, I had a Modern European History teacher who taught in a college style. We had weekly quizzes, but the end of semester exams were the big sink-or-swim events. I'd been out sick and missed the weekly quiz. My teacher kept bugging me about making it up. I hadn't actually read the material and really didn't want to take the time to go back and pick it up either. Finally, I agreed to come in and take the quiz just to have it over with.

As I sat in the empty classroom listening to Mr. Baker read off the quiz questions, I had no clue about any of the answers. After all, you can't "make up" history. So, I decided to do something I'd always wanted to do. I wrote down every funny answer I could think of.

I turned my paper in and watched the expression on his face as he began to shake his head and laugh. He looked up at me and said, "For sense of humor, you get 'A.' For Modern European History, you get 'F.'" Well, that was a forgone conclusion, so I thanked him and left, feeling "Whew, at least that's over with!"

When it was time for our final exam, though, he warned us that we better study! It was going to be a cumulative test. As it turned out, that was an understatement! The final exam was one question—"Write everything you know about Modern European History." Talk about sink-or-swim! You either knew it or you didn't. You could explain it in a logical and connected way or you couldn't.

When it comes to explaining religions, philosophies, or life views like Christianity, it's sometimes difficult to put into words simply because there's always *more*—more to discover, more to learn, more to experience, more to understand, more to put into practice. But the following is an attempt to hit the high points of the most prominent religions and, hopefully, to help you understand the basics.

There are fundamentals and principles in every religion. Some people sort through each one looking for similarities and discovering a few. Each one deals in some way with origin, purpose, morality, and destiny. They all basically affirm doing whatever they think is good while holding out rewards for those who conform, or punishments for those who don't.

For example, Hindus believe in "dharma"—the Eternal Law that propels them toward a self-realization and a final peaceful state, although this may take many reincarnations and depends on adherence to maintaining and following one's basic dharma. It gives complete freedom to explore one's inner world in order to arrive at "Truth." That does not mean that it advocates permissiveness or an incorrect way of life. Demons may lead people in the wrong way.

For the Hindu, life is a battlefield of good and evil, and an individual must observe and protect his dharma and religious laws. If he does not observe his dharma, he is not entitled to *moksha* or salvation. God(s) exist both inside and outside of him. They are spiritual energies that help him to progress towards "*Aditi*," the Light, and attain "*Soma*," the state of divine bliss. It may take many lifetimes to achieve *Soma* and it's a very gradual progression through the caste system of delineated spiritual and social status.

Buddhists believe that the interaction of the five "*skandhas*" create an illusion of "a self." The *skandhas*, which are basically different ways of sensing or perceiving things; and karma, which is the cause and effect of volitional acts; and understanding *dakkha*, which means that "life is suffering, stressful, or unsatisfactory" leaves each person to work out his own state of being.

Mind is chief and the goal is to achieve a degree of harmony with man and nature through a state of consciousness. *Samsara* is the "continuous flow" of the birth, life, death, and reincarnation cycle until the soul is perfected and ends in an ultimate state of bliss. If one is evil, on the other hand, he may reincarnate as an animal or other unfortunate being.

The Four Noble Truths of Buddhism are:

1. Life means suffering.
2. The origin of suffering is attachment.
3. The cessation of suffering is attainable.
4. The path to the cessation of suffering is a gradual path of self-improvement.

Islam consists of six basic beliefs and Allah is the god. The roots of Allah come from an ancient god originally known as Uber. He was the moon god, hence the symbol of Islam is the crescent moon and star. Mohammed referred to him as Aliah, and later, he became known as Allah. Mohammed was attempting originally to counter Judeo or Christian beliefs, and later also to appeal to all religions in a sort of combined image of God. His propelling supernatural experience left questions in his mind as to whether the visions came from "God" or "Satan." But upon discussing them with his older wife, she convinced him of their God-given nature.

Some people assume that Allah is simply another name for the Jewish or Christian God, Yahweh or Jehovah. However, that's not the case.

These are the six basic tenets of Islam:

Shahalah—Allah is the one and only God and Mohammed is his messenger. *Salah*—Prayer five times a day facing Mecca. *Sawm*—Fasting during the month of Ramadan. *Zakat*—Alms giving. *Haji*—A pilgrimage to Mecca (at least once in a lifetime.) And finally, *Jihad*—meaning "to strive or struggle," exerting one's utmost power in contending with an object of disapprobation (the devil, one's own self, or others through personal or military conflict). Killing an infidel (an unbeliever, anyone *not* adhering to Islam) promises seventy-two virgins in the afterlife. Following Sharia law in this way and in all ways insures favor with Allah.

One's reward or punishment depends on how successful one is in keeping the law under the watchful eye of a somewhat distant, rule-oriented god. The extremes under Sharia law are many. Stoning and amputation are often considered proper and deserved punishment. Women are considered property of the man and need a man to supervise and substantiate their daily existence. Mohammed had twelve wives, the youngest of which he married when she was age six, but waited until she was nine to consummate the marriage.

A good Muslim is always striving to master himself through adhering to the strict Sharia law. For a Muslim, the question of "How much good is enough good?" however, becomes a somewhat unknowable yet weighty issue in determining his eternity. Islam teaches that Jesus was a good prophet but Mohammed is the ultimate prophet and the final word. This presents a few problems as Jesus and Mohammed taught different things in some of their basic precepts.

In his book, *Mere Christianity*, the famous author C.S. Lewis argues the impossibility of logic in assuming Jesus was simply a good teacher or prophet. First, that's not what He claimed. He claimed to be *The Only Begotten Son of God*—not *a son* of God, but One with the Father (John 10:30). Jesus said, "I am the way, the truth, and the life: no man cometh unto the Father, but by me" (John 14:6). Lewis proposes that there are only three possible options regarding that claim: He was a liar and He pulled off the biggest scam and hoax the world has ever known; He was a lunatic; *or He was who He said He was.* Those are the only three possible options. "Just a good teacher" is a logical impossibility.

Christians believe that He is who He claimed to be—the son of the living God—God incarnate. Christians believe in the saving grace of Jesus Christ who provides a *personal relationship*; an *indwelling oneness yet otherness*; *forgiveness of sin* (sin being missing God's mark through doing things our own way); and *eternity in the presence of a loving, all-powerful, faithful God.*

Most religions agree about the "being nice" thing

although they have different standards of what that means. It's the "how you become nice" that especially takes different paths.

Christianity is the only religion that is actually more of a relationship than a religion (although many who call themselves Christians may not access that). Other religions are man's attempt to please their gods based on human effort and works. Christianity, however, is simply responding to God's request—first, that we accept what He's already done on our behalf; then, that we become grafted into His family through accepting and appropriating the gift of the Holy Spirit; and finally, that we allow Him to live His life in us and through us. It's His presence that affects our actions when our "I" becomes a "we."

Christianity is dependent on *who God is.* All *other religions* are dependent on *who we are.* One concept is a heart thing—reliant on Jesus Christ and his faithfulness. The other is a performance thing—reliant on how good we can be of our own volition.

There are many wonderful people practicing many different faiths who are trying very hard to do the best they can with what they know or have been taught. On judgment day, when this earth falls from the sky, and each person who has ever lived stands before the Supreme Magistrate of all the universe, they will face not only the God of love but also a God of justice. At that time, everyone—kings and paupers alike—will give account of what they did with what they had, what they knew, and how much they sought to know (Revelation 20:11–15). Man looks on the outside but God looks at the heart (1 Samuel 16:7). There will be no mistakes made on that final day.

Those who have *chosen* the dark side and those who *know* the offer God has made, but have point-blank *refused* it, won't have the "And they lived happily ever after" ending to the story. God's justice will prevail. It's also a choice that forfeits the benefits of having a relationship with God here and now. But for those who know Him and are known by Him, there will be great joy. He will wipe every tear from our eyes and there will be no more pain or suffering (Revelation 21:4).

Other than this brief overview, this book doesn't attempt to explain the many religious routes some explore in looking for God or in trying to find peace. But it does attempt to bring new light to the Christian perspective regarding the common desires of man's heart, and the way God makes provision for those desires and needs. The things that we long for are actually built into the system.

We experience longing *because there is such a thing as love.*

We experience hunger *because there is such a thing as food.*

We experience thirst *because there is such a thing as water.*

We experience the vacancies and fleeting nature of life *because there is such a thing as heaven.*

We experience a desire to live forever *because there is such a thing as eternity.*

We experience cosmic loneliness *because there is such a thing as God.*

Wherever there is an intrinsic need, God gives the supply (Psalm 3: 4–5, Psalm 142, John 6:35).

As previously mentioned, other religions are man's attempt to reach God or to please their gods or to merely attain a state of peaceful consciousness. Christianity, on the other hand, is God's attempt to reach man. He reaches into history with an offer of love, forgiveness, and restoration after mankind has chosen repeatedly to take his own path and go his own way. Yet, as the Creator, He's perfectly entitled to do whatever He wants whether counterintuitive *to us* or not! However unworthy or belligerent we are, it doesn't change who *He is*. He tells us that He is Love…not that He *has* love, but that He *is* Love. It's His very essence.

Through nature, He reveals Himself majestically to everyone, so that no one has an excuse not to "get it." Then, through scripture, He reveals himself more specifically. He tells us things like "I'm here for you. I'm your Father. I created you. I'm making constant provision for you. I love you" (John 1:1–18, John 3:16–17, John 10:28, John 10:30, John 11:25–26). "I want to live my life in you and through you. I want to be with you all the time, with my indwelling presence guiding you" (Matthew 11:27–30/10:29–33, John 10:9–11). "I will never leave you or forsake you" (Hebrews13:5–8). Remember, it's not a religion we're talking about. It's a relationship.

When Christianity becomes a philosophy—just following sets of rules or rituals, celebrations, or traditions—it loses its distinction and falls into the same category as any other religion. Christianity is alive. *Jesus Christ*, the heavenly ambassador, *was a radical*. He confronted the religious men of His day and called them whited sepulchers (whitewashed tombs). He overthrew the money changers tables in the temple and said, "You have made my Father's house of prayer into a den of thieves" (Matthew 21:13, paraphrased). He was bold, but He was good. He was loving, yet He was just. He was miraculous, but He was simple. He died, but now He's alive... forever alive! And He offers us eternal life too.

So, that's the person this narrative is based on. Why did Jesus do what He did? Why does His life, right out of the gates, seem a little bizarre in spots? Perhaps it's because the Father who sent Him says, "For my thoughts *are* not your thoughts, neither *are* your ways my ways, saith the Lord. For *as* the heavens are higher than the earth, so are my ways higher than your ways, and my thoughts than your thoughts" (Isaiah 55:8–9).

I hope you enjoy the following account regarding our search. But, before we begin, let's look at the foundation upon which this belief system is based. It's that "looking for truth" thing.

Something to Think About:

If you were making up your own "religion", which would you likely come up with—a "religion" where you are responsible for reaching up to God or a "religion" where God reaches down to you?

As a human being, what reasons can we give for why God should be the one to provide the love, forgiveness, and restoration parts of the relationship . . . or, even for that matter, why God should desire to have a relationship with each of us at all?

Is it obvious that Christianity is not the sort of idea that most people would come up with on their own?

If you consider yourself a Christian, how's your relationship with Jesus going? Have you ever possibly switched the premise of your faith to basically being one of works rather than trust?

CHAPTER THREE

Why Do You Think That?

WHY DO YOU THINK THAT?

I remember hearing the story of a kid who lived out in the country and had discovered a pipe that extended up from a septic tank. Out playing one day, he and a buddy decided to light a match, throw it down the hole, and see what would happen.

Well, of course, all @#%&$ broke loose. The gases ignited, fire shot back up the pipe, and his eyebrows and hair caught on fire. He ran for home crying and screaming in pain. His mom took an aloe leaf and covered the burns on his head and face.

That same boy later grew up to be a research doctor. He developed a special treatment for burns and comprehensive cellular health based on his childhood

prank and the healing power of aloe that he'd personally experienced.

Sometimes, it's the trials that cause pain through
which we discover ultimate answers. And, sometimes,
we have to make mistakes to discover what doesn't
work before we find out what does.

Along the way, I've made a lot of mistakes. I've
heard all sorts of doctrine and struggled with some.
I've learned from great teachers, but still spent years
searching for truth. It's been an intense growing process, through deep waters and consuming fires … and
I still learn more every day. The master craftsman, the
potter, isn't finished with me yet. But ultimately, I've
come to understand that the essence of Christianity
comes from understanding one basic concept. This
precept is based on "the breath of God." It's the
greatest "how-to" part of our faith.

Do you like old hymns? Maybe not…. Okay, I
confess, I like them. There's one that goes, "Breathe
on me Breath of God. Fill me with Life anew. That

I may love what thou doest love and do what thou wouldst do."

I know, we don't talk that way anymore, but the words of the old hymn are still true. What does it mean to be filled with the "breath of God," though? What's it talking about? We'll come back to this. But first, in looking for an answer, we need to find a reliable source. We need something that's more than just guessing.

The source Christians use is the Bible. The Bible is the most scrutinized and the most examined book in history. Even those who have tried to discredit it have admitted the unusual high adherence to textual criticism in confirming over ninety-five percent agreement verified by original documents, and written within a time period where firsthand public witnesses were still alive.

The Bible is not actually just one book but rather a compilation of sixty-six books containing history, poetry, prophecy, letters, philosophy, and eschatology. It was written over the course of 1,500 years by forty different authors from shepherds, fishermen, and prophets, to doctors, kings, and family members. Most of these authors didn't know each other and never collaborated…yet they agreed. This book was written on three different continents, in three different languages—Hebrew, Greek, and Aramaic—yet the various accounts verify each other. The story line is contiguous and follows a theme. It's a flowing commentary on the creation, the fall, God's redemption, universal love for all of mankind, salvation for those willing to turn around and give up control, transformation for those willing to relinquish their core beings to God, and purpose in becoming ambassadors on earth and living in His presence for eternity.

As a professor once challenged his students, I would challenge anyone to produce sixty-six books written on any subject, by forty different authors, on three different continents, in three different languages, over a period of 1,500 years, with a common storyline, in perfect agreement, and with no historical errors. If anyone can do that, I guess I might have to admit that there isn't anything so unusual, supernatural, or "God-breathed" about the Bible either.

Take, for example, in the examination of someone like Aristotle. His life and teachings are not questioned even though the documentation of his life and sayings are miniscule next to the thousands of verified records we have of the life and teachings of Jesus, including those from both biblical and secular historians such as the famous Josephus and Suetonius.

Cultures of the time often handed down information from generation to generation through oral tradition. But in the case of Jesus, it was written down as well, all close to the time of the events, and communicated by those with firsthand experience. They'd been there!

Have you ever played that game where one person starts a rumor and then it's whispered to another person in the room until it finally comes back to the person who started it? Usually, by the time it gets back, it's unrecognizable. People use this example sometimes to suggest that you can't rely on biblical accuracy. They say something like "After all, look at the different translations. It's been adjusted throughout the years time and again. And with the input of so many people, it has to be much like the whispering game." Therefore, they dismiss it. However, in the case of the Bible, this couldn't be further from the truth.

Regarding attention to editorial details, my sister-in-law is a medical illustrator. A lot of attention to accuracy is necessary in checking the specimen used, comparing and studying other available drawings, as well as coordinating with the author whose work is also repeatedly checked, updated, and verified from many sources. But the verification of scientists, authors, editors, and illustrators, with procedures to catch any of the tiniest errors, doesn't come anywhere near the scrutiny that has repeatedly and continually been given to the Scripture over the course of hundreds of years.

In biblical studies, not just a few editors but thousands of scholars have both verified it and attempted to discredit it. However, the more it's examined, the more its accuracy is confirmed. Often in places where historical accuracy has been questioned, some honest scrutiny uncovers that the Bible is, in fact, correct in the end. Other supposed contradictions occur when passages are lifted out of context and then compared. The point of the real message is missed. Not a matter of contradiction but of misunderstanding and misinterpretation by the reader.

With the discovery of the Dead Sea Scrolls in 1947 and the continuing excavation through 1956, suspected modern errors or changes were once again debunked as these ancient documents verified concurrency with the textual accuracy of today's Old Testament scriptures to approximate 94% agreement. And the small differences are not regarding anything significant to the meaning. These scrolls written by the Essenes and hidden away in caves just outside of Jerusalem were sealed in jars and date back to between 200 B.C. to 68 C.E./A.D. They show Christianity's roots in Judaism and have proven a significant link between the Old and New Testaments.

Modern translations sometimes lose the richness and pictures originally conveyed, but the overall truth remains even if simplified or with less color. For a more significant understanding, it's good to study the scriptures with a Greek/Aramaic and Hebrew Lexicon in hand. The finer points show up in the original written language. But the evidence substantiates that the information given in our Bible has been studied under a magnifying glass, *figuratively and literally*, and verified. In cases where there's a lack of deeper completeness through attempts at modernization, a technical language study always clarifies, amplifies, and verifies the meaning.

Here's another interesting observation regarding biblical authenticity. Most often, accounts are written from the perspective of the "winners." When people are part of the story they're telling, they usually like to come off looking good. But in this case, the story is told from the perspective of the "losers." For example, Jesus' friends and disciples writing their stories relayed what they'd seen and heard, but included their own fear and disillusionment. Why would the storytellers admit that they doubted, that they were cowards, that they ran, that they betrayed, that they had been—at times—on the wrong side of the issues… unless it was true? The fact of the matter was that their dreams had been shattered. Jesus' disciples and followers were looking for a political leader as well as a spiritual leader. They expected Jesus to end the Roman oppression and set up His kingdom in a physical sense. And now He was dead! Their enemies had won. They were reeling and they admitted it. It took a while for things to change. Even when the women reported that they'd seen Jesus and that He was alive again, the disciples didn't believe them.

This is another example of the truth of the story. If they were making it up or embellishing the story, they certainly would *not* have had *women* reporting the resurrection! And they certainly would *not* have had the reports *not* being believed! They would have had *men* telling the story and the story *being* believed.

In that day, a woman's testimony wasn't admissible in court. It carried no weight at all. So, it would make no sense to make up a story they intended to be credible while, at the same time, including the part about women reporting it. They told it that way because it happened that way! Also, in this case, the disciples themselves didn't believe the women until they saw Him for themselves. All of the pieces of the puzzle correlate to a genuine description of reality and a normal response for that time in history. It reeks of truth! As a matter of fact, even after the reports of both the women and the other disciples, the apostle Thomas said, "I won't believe it until I see the scars and touch the wound" (John 20:25). When it comes right down to it, most of us pride ourselves on our skepticism. We're too smart to be taken in! And so it was with them.

Consider this anecdote: When my little brother was five, we lived in southeastern Ohio in a neighborhood that was tiered up the side of a mountain. We'd only lived there a short time when he came home with a great story about a big Indian village that was in the woods at the dead end of the street. Hmmm…. He told us about a teepee and the covered wagon and totem pole and various other interesting inventions of his active imagination. No one believed him. Actually, I thought his description was pretty good. And he seemed very excited about it if it was just made up. It couldn't be real, though...could it?

One afternoon, I decided to check it out. I went down to the end of the street and started climbing up the steep incline through the woods to where he'd said it was. And what do you think I found? An Indian village! It was exactly like he said it was! There, in front of me, was everything he'd described. As I began to explore the area with the covered wagon and teepee, someone approached, walking down the mountainside.

"Do you like my Indian village?" the man asked.

"Yeah. It's great," I answered. "Did you make all of this?"

"I did. I thought the neighborhood kids might like it. I guess I've got a little American pioneer in my blood."

I finished my talk with the man (a professor in town at Ohio University, I assumed) and ran home. I burst through the door yelling, "Randy's right! There's an Indian village at the end of the street just like he said!"

When someone claims something that people can either validate or easily discredit, they would do well to keep it to themselves unless they're telling the truth. So it was with the disciples. There were many people around who were witnesses to the events as well as to their claims regarding the events.

The fact of the matter was that, when they reversed themselves, they were putting their own lives in jeopardy *by claiming He was alive.* They were subjecting themselves not only to ridicule but to death. They were making themselves part of something considered as not only religious insurrection but political insurrection. Yet they held to the story. People don't intentionally fabricate things to make themselves look ridiculous and get themselves killed. Someone may die for something he believes in, but he won't die for something he knows he made up.

The biblical account simply has the ring of truth. All of the warts and flaws have been hung out for everyone to see. It's totally *not* written in the way that self-glorifying made-up stories or myths are written. But whether you adhere to the Bible or not, try to hang in there with me for a few more pages…just in case there might be some truth to it.

As previously mentioned, while many scholars have affirmed its veracity and historicity, experience has proven its claims for me. So, I ask you to examine some biblical teachings because, without biblical credibility, there is no Christianity.

I realize that even some who consider themselves Christians only believe parts of the Bible. They pick and choose. Anything miraculous or out of the norm like the Adam and Eve account, the virgin birth, or the resurrection, etc., they just wink at. But the Bible claims that *"All scripture is given by inspiration of God and is profitable for doctrine, for reproof, for correction, for instruction in righteousness" (2 Timothy 3:16).*

Is that part of the "throwaway" scripture? Again, it comes back to who and what you're going to believe. What is true and what is truth? For me, a God who can create the universe with all of its galaxies and planets, and the world with all of its forms of life and intricate systems all in balance, can do anything he wants. He's not restricted to my finite thinking or actions. It baffles me how anyone can scrutinize nature and come to the conclusion that it's the result of some cosmic accident or happenstance or just a really, really, really, really long time!

Really?!

If God wants to create through a virgin birth, that's not hard for him. It's only impossible for us. If He wants to create the world through speaking it into existence, that's not hard for Him. It's only impossible for us.

If you look at the miracles of nature and see no evidence of a Divine Creator, if you consider all the magnificent complexities and still see only accidents of evolution, then I confess you have more faith than I do. That's a leap I can't make.

With the science of today, the *"theory* of evolution" has basically broken down although not often reported. In some cases, it has also been exposed as not an accident of misinterpreting evidence but of intentionally misrepresenting evidence. Even Darwin himself stated that his theory was wrong if it was found that there is no increase of information in genomes during the progression of evolution. The mutation of a species consistently renders it in a compromised state that is *not* sustained in mating. Test tube experiments produce species that may survive in the laboratory but are repeatedly eliminated in nature. Science, to this day, cannot produce substantiated evidence of macroevolution (one species changing into another). Despite the missing links and weak links perpetrated as facts in our educational systems, any substantiated evidence of evolution is merely microevolution—another name for adaptation. In those instances, when the environment reverts to its original state, so does the species.

The species, during the adaptation process of microevolution, contain less information in the genome, which negates Darwin's theory by his own words. The adapted species, in every case, is a mutant version of the original in a weakened state and cannot endure the survival of the fittest.

Irreducible complexity and other scientific discoveries, in light of DNA examination, and things like the "God particle" continue to uncover evidence of creation and other facts that have rendered the random selection of evolution indefensible by many current scientists (but that's another book). The fact is that we all have the same science. Science is not what's in question. We agree on the science (except in cases where it has been intentionally misinterpreted or skewed, i.e., Hegel's embryos). Where the disagreement comes is in the interpretation of the science. It comes back to philosophy...world view...theology.

It would seem that evolutionists are clouded by their own agenda and worldview, maybe even more conclusively than the creationists they accuse of the same. After all, if monkeys are our ancestors then we answer to no one. We are, in essence, our own gods. If God, however, is our Father/Creator, then we answer to Him. (Have you ever asked yourself, "If apes turn into people, why are there still apes?")

When you come right down to it, isn't the argument really about philosophy and theology?

The Bible explains that we're created in God's image, not the other way around. If we were creating God in our image, we *would* create Him based on *our* idea of impressiveness, benevolence, fairness, and justice. He would be the nice grandfather in the sky who set the clock ticking, provides constant treats, never punishes us, fixes all of our tickets, erases all of our mistakes, and takes no notice of our abuses—all without us ever having to answer to Him or even acknowledge Him for that matter. Then He'd see how we did when the party's over. But it wouldn't really matter. Everyone's going home with a prize, regardless! But God's plan is different from that. He didn't want to raise a bunch of spoiled brats who didn't even *want* to know Him.

What man would have ever thought up the ideas explained in scripture? None of us! Who would have thought up the idea of a God reaching down to us? Who would have thought up Him personally making the sacrifice we owe, being the stand-in for our rebellion and messes, our self-serving hearts, and bad attitude? That's not our nature! There's something inside us that wants to feel worthy, to pay our own way besides the opposite thing we have going on where we want to be excused from accountability. Left to our own devices, we'd choose to make our own decisions and never suffer the consequences. We'd claim the credit but never the blame—want the independence but not the accountability.

In the scriptures, God tells us that being adopted and loved by Him isn't based on what we do or our worthiness. It's based on who He is and His worthiness. *It's not about who we are! It's about who He is!*

What? Who on earth would come up with that? This is good news that's preposterous! His proposal of love (and adoption) is outrageous! Besides which, He loves all the wrong people! Jesus, who was the actual Creator (with the Father and the Spirit), the One who walked with Adam and Eve in the Garden, loved us enough to die for us "while we were yet sinners." (He was famous for hanging out with and loving the wrong crowd.) And that's one of the very reasons why it has to be true. It's totally out of the scope of man to invent something that improbable. It's not the way our minds work.

The philosophical and mental chasm between who He is and who we are is extreme, not to speak of the scientific chasm. If it's not easy for you to see the chasm, maybe you'd like to create a blade of grass out of nothing today, or maybe you'd rather be in charge of coordinating sunsets?

Our love will never be as complete as His, our greatness will never be as big as His, and our assignments and responsibilities will never be as comprehensive as His. But we're still created in His image. We have much more access to the power and life He intends to exhibit through us than most of us realize. What we need to do is to move it from our heads to our hearts and use what we've been given!

So…who are we? And who is God? And what is His real plan for our interaction and union?

Something to Think About:

What difference would it make in your approach to life if man was simply an accident of nature and evolved from an ape, versus being created by an all-powerful, loving God?

What is the importance of considering the Scripture as the God-breathed, inspired word of God?

Do you think that having sixty-six books written by forty different authors, on three different continents, in three different languages, over a period of 1,500 years, and all agreeing and corroborating each other's stories is an unusual feat?

Have you ever thought about the fact that the Bible is written from the perspective of not only the eye-witnesses but also of the "betrayers?" If you were writing a story that you were the star of, do you think you'd tell it with all the flaws hung out to dry?

CHRISTIANITY:
WHAT'S THE BIG DEAL?

CHRISTIANITY:
WHAT'S THE BIG DEAL?

J esus told lots of stories and often spoke in parables. So, I'm going to try to explain Christianity in sort of a narrative way, interjecting stories and insights.

Unlike fairy tales, the story doesn't open with "Once upon a time." It opens with, "In the beginning." Is God good or what? He wants us to know the story from the very beginning! The first serious question almost every child asks is, "Where did I come from?" So, God sets off to give us the answer.

I'm reminded of the story of a little boy going to

his mom one day, asking her that question. "Where did I come from, Mom?"

The mother's wheels were spinning. She hadn't expected that question to come so early. But she did her best to go into a long and tactful explanation.

After she finished, her son looked at her with a puzzled look and said, "No Mom, I didn't mean like all that stuff. I meant like Timmy said he came from Cincinnati."

(Sorry. Couldn't resist.)

Anyway, the story starts at the beginning. And it's a great start with God thinking of everything— Him being all love, totally creative, all-knowing, and all-powerful. He speaks everything into existence and provides man with everything He could possibly want or need. And He commands each species to reproduce *"after its own kind"* (Genesis 1:24).

Back in the late seventies, I worked for an organization that often hosted famous people. The president had bought a few beautiful homes surrounding the main complex where the guests would stay for the duration of their visit. Limousines whisked in and out, taking them to each appointment, interview, or television appearance. The cupboards and refrigerator were always stocked with fresh treats and staples. Anything that anyone could want was anticipated and provided. Talk about royal treatment! But it doesn't even compare with God's provisions in the Garden of Eden. (Eden meaning *pleasure*.)

God began by creating the Garden of Pleasure. There was no running through the rain to get into a limo in the Garden of Pleasure. Adam and Eve had been given the perfect climate and never needed to rush anywhere. They had no pressure of interviews, making good impressions, or deadlines. They had perfect bodies, perfect relationships, wonderful food, and beauty growing all around them. And the one who talked with them and escorted them daily was the Creator of the universe, God Himself.

In the first and second chapters of Genesis, it says explicitly that Elohim created man in His image. He designed us to carry His fingerprint. He made us in

His likeness. We've been created to be just like our Dad—to have His eyes, His ears, His heart, His mind. Then, He honored mankind with responsibility. "Care for my creation. I give you dominion over it all," He proclaimed. Can you imagine making something as magnificent as the earth and everything in it, and then turning it all over to someone else to take care of and enjoy? That's what I call trust!

In Genesis 2:19, He told Adam, "Whatever you want to name everything, is okay with me." What honor! What friendship! What ownership! Can you imagine the creator of the Indian village saying to my brother and me, "What do you want to call this place? I'm giving it to you. You take care of it for me and enjoy it however you want. I want you to name everything I've put here too. I trust you to take care of it. There are lots of animals that come and go here. You're in charge. Name them and care for them. It's all yours." Wow! I can't even imagine the generosity and demonstration of confidence that would take. Actually, it might have been a little overwhelming for a couple of kids, unless the builder of the village also said, "And I'll be right here to answer your questions and help you." But that's the generosity and confidence, the sort of relationship God shared with Adam and Eve. He didn't leave them alone with all of it. He blessed them with His presence, walking and talking with them, being there for them daily. He evidently really liked being with them and vice versa. They shared everything!

Here's the thing, though. You can *give without loving,* but you can't *love without giving.* Love isn't love if it's demanded. Love loses its essence without choice. So, God also gave them choice—freewill.

I remember a seventh-grade teacher of mine who made some bad choices. He used to mutter to himself a lot. He yelled a lot too. He hit kids with yardsticks or, sometimes, put them under his desk and kicked them. And he really didn't know much about the subjects he was trying to teach either. It was sort of a disastrous year. But, regardless of his behavior, the one thing that he always demanded was "respect!" He didn't give respect but he attempted to bluster and scare everyone into giving it to him. It didn't work. I didn't know why he couldn't understand that respect isn't demanded, it's earned. Sure, you can beat people into submission, but you can't *make* them respect you.

It won't work to demand love either. It's that inside heart thing again. And so it was then that God established freedom right from the start. He ordained choice. He provided opportunity and demonstrated love. But He didn't demand it back. With the availability of choice, in time, Adam and Eve made some bad ones. They bought into the deceiver's lies. They believed the slander the serpent sowed—that God really didn't have their best interest in mind; that God was keeping good things from them; that God just didn't want to share the glory. They believed the deception. They bought into the idea that choosing the fruit from the *Tree of the Knowledge of Good and Evil* would simply make them like God. After all, what could be bad about being like God?

The fact was that they were choosing *to be* God, to decide for themselves what was good and bad, to be in charge, to be on their own. In short, they chose to *not* believe God and *not* trust Him with their lives. They, in essence, decided to replace God with themselves.

The battle for "godhead" is always control. And don't we all struggle with that same choice today?

"Mine!" is a favorite word in each child's vocabulary. A favorite sentence of little ones is usually something like "Do it own self." And, as we age, it continues. Statistically, eighty-five percent of all arguments, or wars for that matter, have at their core level a struggle over "Who gets to say?" "Whose way is it going to be done?" "Ultimately, who's in control?" And that battle goes all the way back to the beginning of time.

In the Garden, they chose to shift their trust and grab control. Theologians refer to this incident as *The Fall* or *Original Sin.* It's part of the trickle-down effect for us today. Man's bent toward not trusting God's plan, word, or provision is insidious. We'd rather trust ourselves.

Would you and I have made the same choice they did? I think we would have, because we obviously make it in some way every day. We wrestle for control on a regular basis. We elevate ourselves to the throne. Dethroning God and replacing Him with self is "sin." It's an insult to God. And it's done out of consummate unbelief. It's like having the guests arrive at the beautiful guest home all prepared for them and them sticking up their noses. It's like them choosing to find their own accommodations, rent their own car, and buy their own food. A foolish choice and an insult to the host who has prepared and provided everything. We still believe the lie that God isn't really good, that somehow, He's going to "gyp" us, and that, ultimately, He doesn't have our best interest in mind. So, we go off on our own.

Sin (capital "S") is always the result of unbelief. And it always results in acts of self. It shows up as self-protecting, self-serving, self-aggrandizing, self-absorbed, self-important, self-interested, selfishness. Selfishness, in turn, produces arrogant (little "s") sins that people try to categorize, prioritize, label, and correct. But think of this, the Lord says, "He who is guilty in one point, is guilty in all" (James 2:10). That doesn't seem quite fair, does it? How can that be? How can murder and gossip be in the same category? That can't be right, can it? But it is—because God sees our heart. He knows that, whether you kill someone with insinuations and attacks that emotionally stop their heart or stick the knife in physically, the root is still the same. The heart motivation is the same. Personal interest and arrogance are in charge. Selfishness, judgment, revenge, and pride have been crowned.

Check it out. Sin always proceeds from the root of self. All resulting sins originate and feed off of desires or calculations we think are in our own best interest and in our own hands. List them if you want. All sins come from a choice that basically says, "I don't want to trust you with this, God. I'll find my own way to meet my own needs because I really don't think you're going to do it...well, not the way it should be done anyway. I doubt that you're really all that loving, wise, or just after all, God. You must not be able to see what's really going on here or you'd let these people have it! Excuse me if I just take care of this myself. I think you don't really like me, do you, God?" These are the kinds of conversations we internalize if we're honest, aren't they?

It's easy for people to take things into their own hands, become the accusers of God, and resemble the father of lies more than the real Father.

Lives become tangled webs of frustration, loneliness, and various forms of disaster because the deceiver's lies, accusations, suggestions, and attacks have been mistaken for truth. We *all* get bombarded with lies and misleading information. Through media and advertisers alone, we experience masters of suggestion and manipulation.

I remember when I was young watching TV ads for Ultra Brite toothpaste. It suggested that, if you used it, you automatically had sex appeal. The opposite sex would be helpless not to fall at your feet, and you'd live happily ever after. Just buy the toothpaste.

What?! How dumb did they think we were? But being cleverly presented, the mental picture and their advertising jingle remains with me these many years later.

Like Adam and Eve, we get seduced into tasting the fruit and believing the suggestions. Any thought that promises our own autonomy, our own right to design life, and our own ability to make the choices that seem to be in our own best interest is appealing. When we stop to realize who we are compared with the great, omniscient, omnipotent, omnipresent God of the universe, we might consider abdicating and letting the real King take the throne.

The true King promises, "My thoughts toward you are for good and not evil to give you a future and hope" (Jeremiah 33:6). How everything unfolds is designed to be in His hands, not ours. Again, Adam and Eve's sin was the same as ours today—*unbelief.* Admittedly, it may seem more natural to trust ourselves. It's easy to believe the lie that started in the Garden—i.e., God doesn't really care and doesn't have our best interest at heart. Most of us truly do want to be in charge of our own accommodations and provisions. We want to earn and control our own destiny. Like Job, we're sure we're getting unfairly besieged and we stand in our own self-righteousness, feeling we're more fair and better than God. We want answers! And the reply to us remains the same as it was to Job—"Where were you when I created the earth and flung the stars into the skies?" So, when Job lost everything, he got an answer to his accusations toward God, which he hadn't expected. In his grief, he'd cried out against his loss and questioned God. But that wasn't the end of the story. Ultimately, God was faithful and restored everything to him in double. God hadn't caused the loss. Satan had. The devil was simply up to his normal tricks and Job's trials were a test.

In our daily lives, though, "When you're up to your eyeballs in alligators, it's sometimes difficult to remember that the purpose was to drain the swamp." When your mind is crying out in pain, who are you going to trust? What are you going to believe in?

Do we dare trust God's word
and His faithfulness?

How can we get things back to the way God has originally intended? Can we really trust Him to bring good out of what seems bad to us? How can we get the crown back to the rightful King?

Back to the story. In the Garden of Eden, the situation was still unfolding. Adam and Eve were given just one instruction—"Don't eat the fruit of the one tree in the middle of the garden, *The Tree of the Knowledge of Good and Evil.*" That was it. There was only one rule…only one thing on the entire face of the earth that was off limits. And they blew it!

The first question that may have popped into their minds was, "Why not?"

"Because then you will surely die," He told them, undoubtedly knowing what was going on in their heads. The death He was referring to was the severing of spiritual oneness they enjoyed with Him and, ultimately, their physical lives as well since they had been created to be eternal beings.

The point was, He didn't want them to

die—spiritually or physically! He didn't want the relationship wrecked. He loved them, so He warned them. But as soon as the deceiver, the sly serpent, came around, they believed the slander. Satan inferred that God was misleading them; that God was trying to keep something good from them; that God was jealous for His position of superiority.

In his slippery questions to Eve, Satan impugned the whole nature of God. He *was* then, as he *is* now, the accuser of God and the accuser of God's kids. Adam and Eve fell for it then. We fall for it now!

It's funny when a toddler covers his own eyes and thinks no one can see him. Adam and Eve's attempts at hiding were almost as comical, even if slightly more creative, in their camouflage fig-leaf outfits. Guilt and hiding go hand in hand. Guilt always results in the same thing—separation. True then, and true today.

But no one can hide from God, no matter how much they might want to.

"What have you done?" God simply says to Eve as the two are discovered. She slip-slides around blaming Satan and claiming that she was tricked (Genesis 3:13).

When the conversation is turned toward Adam, he blames both God and Eve.

"The *woman You gave me*, gave the fruit to me and I did eat" (Genesis 3:12, author's paraphrase). Not his fault! God's fault because He gave the woman to him and she gave him the fruit.

One of the funniest things to me is that we still use the same excuses today. When a woman screws up, it's usually because she got tricked, she got deceived. "The lady in the store said it looked good on me. How could I know your grandmother has a dress just like it?" Or, "The mechanic said the car needed a new transmission. How could I know it was just low on fluid?" She got flimflammed!

Men, on the other hand, always have to do *whatever* to please someone else—their wife, their kids, the boss, etc. It's always someone else's fault. "I had to lie because the boss expected me to make the sale." "I had to cheat on my taxes if I'm going to take my wife on that trip she's expecting."

Even though He already knew the answers, God asked the two of them a few simple questions to help them face the truth. Yet they blamed everyone but themselves. Already, the self-interest and self-protection were openly on display. The choices they made had necessary consequences. It was inevitable. They had to leave the Garden. Why? Because there was another tree in the Garden called *The Tree of Life*. If they ate the fruit of *that tree* then, they'd live forever in an eternal existence, but separated from God and everything good permanently. Out of His love, He could not take a chance on them making another bad choice. The chance had to be subverted by distancing them from the option. There are always consequences, good or bad, that come with choices. Can you imagine the grief they felt? Can you just hear them blaming each other because they both bought the suggestions hook, line, and sinker? They both tried eating from *The Tree of the Knowledge of Good and Evil*, thinking they would become as God, equal with Him. They were equally guilty.

In reality, they thought it sounded perfectly

reasonable and good to replace God's sovereignty with their own. Who they were created to be versus who they chose to be was a great fall. What they were created to be and what they chose to be were very different and massively less.

Years ago a TV game show started called "Let's Make a Deal." People in the audience would make deals and trade what they'd brought to the show, or something they'd already won, for what was behind a curtain or in a box. At the end of the show, there was always "the big deal." This was the final trade and one lucky contestant got to trade something they won that was really good for a gamble at something spectacular. On the other hand, it could also be something worthless ... "a zonk."

Sometimes, people lost the good thing they already had and got "zonked." Other times, they won the big prize, something really awesome. But there was always a consequence to their choice. In Adam and Eve's case, they chose *the zonk*. They'd already been told what was behind the curtains and in the boxes. But they ignored it. Once a shadow was cast on the trustworthiness of the original information, they chose against the One who had always been faithful and went instead with their own instincts under the influence of the adversary.

God had breathed life into them. In God's deal, they shared life and likeness with Him. Can't you just see Adam coming alive with the Zoë breath of God filling him? The Hebrew word for "breathed" here means "a mighty blast." It was, in essence, the first mouth-to-mouth resuscitation that brought man to life and filled him. Adam was filled with the breath of God...God's oxygen giving life...His dazzling presence...His Zoë.

Although not stated directly, being created in God's image may be assumed to originally also contain His light; being clothed in light, so to speak. We know from several references, especially Paul's encounter on the Damascus road or Moses' encounter on the mount, that God's presence is one of extreme radiance.

The scriptures reveal to us in many places that

God's essence is an incredibly brilliant light. His first words of creation were "Let there be light." Jesus continually calls Himself the Light of the world. So, were Adam and Eve clothed in light as God is? I believe it's logical to assume they were. But when self was placed in control, when trust was broken, when the Spirit of God was quenched inside of them, *the lights went out.* No longer covered and filled with God's light, they saw themselves as they really were ... alone and naked. What a huge absence! No wonder they felt exposed. No wonder they cringed at being naked. No wonder they wanted to hide.

They had been created to live forever with God's light shining in them, through them, and surrounding them. But His light in them was now extinguished. Yet, in His mercy, God chose to reach out again. A new plan was set in motion.

The first thing on God's agenda was to replace the uncomfortable, impractical leaf attire with comfortable, long-lasting leather wear. It would be a poor substitute for being clothed in His light, but it was a great improvement over their own fig-leaf fashion!

After all, they were going to be living in the desert (East of Eden). Not a good climate for total exposure!

Now, the sacrifice of an innocent animal had to be made in order to create new outfits to keep them protected in the new world they were about to encounter. Their guilt-ridden, inadequate, in-hiding, self-made camouflage clothes could be thrown away. They were being re-clothed, covered once again by God's loving provision, even in the face of their broken trust and rebellion. What love!

So, from the beginning, blood was shed as God sacrificed an innocent one to create a necessary covering. And it was all caused by the sin of their unprovoked *unbelief.* In the face of His goodness and trustworthiness, His provision and protection, His love and relationship, His wisdom and integrity, they'd chosen to *not believe* Him and to go on their own.

Nevertheless, He continued to love them enough to cover the shame of their choice. Their shame was not in the nakedness of their bodies, *it was in the absence of His Light.* They made their choice. It was *a zonk* of their own choosing. And their attempt at the old cover-up was really lame.

And so it was then that the practice of sacrificing an innocent—"the shedding of blood for the remission (covering) of sin"—continued through the ages until, by the time of Christ, there was quite an extensive system developed for all the different sacrifices to be made. And all were made in remembrance of, and in extension of, that first sacrifice.

Eventually, priests were set in place to be the representatives—representing the people before God. And the people were instructed to always bring their very best to the Lord for the burnt offering (barbeque) because the sacrifice, in most cases, was later eaten by those making the sacrifice. When God cooks dinner, He intends to serve the very best.

"I shall be your God and you shall be my people," God promised the children of Israel. The word *shall* is a present continuous tense. Isn't that great? It's not a promise for the future. It's not a promise just for the moment. It's a promise for now and forever.

In the Old Covenant, He continued reminding

them of His promise by establishing the sacrificial system so that there would be specific and tangible occurrences for not forgetting all that had taken place from the beginning. The protection and provision that began in the Garden, continued. As it had first become necessary to create a new covering for the naked result of sin, so the sin offering for the children of Israel continued to be a demonstration of forgiveness, love, provision, and covering. The sin offering was a twofold procedure in which a lamb would be sacrificed as a "burnt offering," but a goat would also be sacrificed as the actual "sin offering." Ceremonially, they would lay the sins of the nation on the goat. The goat would then be released into the desert to carry away the sins of the people. *That's where we get the term "scapegoat."* So, then, what happened to the goat? Well, it would die. And after it died, then what happened? It would be devoured by scavengers.

Do you see the picture that's being drawn here? Any attempt to revisit the past sin had been wiped out. There was no way to find it again. It was gone! Swallowed up!

I heard a story once of a little girl who was becoming known around her church as someone who actually talked with God and heard back from Him. The pastor, thinking that he didn't want this to get out of hand, started a conversation with the little girl one morning as she was leaving.

"I understand you talk with God and He talks back to you?" he began.

"Yes," she nodded innocently.

"Well, the next time you talk with Him, ask Him what my last sin was, okay?"

"Okay," she said. Then she smiled and walked away.

The next Sunday, as she was leaving again, the pastor said, "Well, did you talk with God this week?"

"Yes," she said.

"Did you ask Him what my last sin was?" he asked.

"Yes," she said.

"Well, what did He say?" he continued.

"He said, 'I forgot.'"

God promises that He buries our sin in the deepest sea and looks on it no more. It's gone as surely as the scapegoat! (Micah 7:18–19) It's impossible to reclaim, even though the accuser may encourage us to endlessly try. The Bible tells us that *Christ* came to take away the sins of the world. He is the *Scapegoat as well as the Lamb*, out of His own willingness and love. He came as "the *propitiation* for our sin." Propitiation...a big word, huh? It simply means an atoning victim, one who makes amends, restitution (Romans 3:25, John 2:2, 1John 4:10). In His mercy and goodness, He's got us covered.

Many religions today practice various tangible ways of trying to make restitution. Rituals, offerings, denials, punishments, self-flagellations, and separation from the material world are all efforts to control destiny, assuage guilt, and somehow ascribe worthiness.

But God had a better plan...

I think, to comprehend the plan, we have to see just how a covenant was made in the Old Testament days. In fact, without understanding the old, it's hard to comprehend the new.

According to history, a covenant was very different from a mere agreement like what we might negotiate between countries or people today. Rather, it was *an imposition* of the greater on the lesser. For example, a greater king would stipulate, "I will do this, and you will do that." The lesser king would then either agree to the imposition or not. Typically, each nation would choose a representative. The representative would stand for all the people. Whatever he said, they said. Whatever he did, they did.

When a covenant was consummated, people from each nation would typically go into an open field. Then, the two representatives would stand in the middle of it where an animal (in most cases a calf) had been slain— the head cut off and the body split in two. Both representatives would literally stand in the middle of this bloody mess to make a covenant.

"Why?" you might ask. "That sounds pretty gory!" Yes, it was. But it carried a lot of significance. By that ritual, they were saying, "If I break this covenant, you can cut off my head, split me in two, and leave me out for the birds just like this animal." Then each representative would make a cut some place on his right forearm and they would press the wounds together, mixing the blood, and thereby proclaiming to all, "We are one in this agreement. This covenant is unto death! From here on, I am for you and you are for me."

When "the manifestation of the Godhead bodily" arrived through Jesus Christ, God initiated a New Covenant. Jesus became the representative, both from the man side and the God side. Not only that, but He became the sacrifice as well—the final sacrifice available for all of mankind. It was a covenant for all time. And it's still in effect today.

It's like He's offered to be our blood brother…He's our representative from the man side in covenant with the God of the Universe, the Supreme Magistrate, the

Omniscient Holy One, the Great I Am. And He's also our representative from the God side. When we agree to this covenant, it means, "I am for you and you are for me even unto death."

The King declares, "This is the New Covenant. Here are the terms: I have your back. I provide for your every need. I'm always here for you. I call you son/daughter, and you call me Abba Father (Daddy). I honor you with responsibilities, caring for my creation and for each other. And I forgive your sins and unbelief. I restore you to the relationship I intended, in total union with Me. I've made a new covering for you. Through the shed blood of Jesus, you are given His new covering as the light of the world, with my indwelling Spirit as your life. Divine light will once again shine through you and blot out all of your transgressions. And, finally, I'll walk and talk with you every day. We'll enjoy constant communication and communion.

"So, what's your part? You love Me and unite with Me and honor Me. You have no other gods before Me. You thank Me, listen to Me, follow My lead, accept My forgiveness, enjoy the attributes inherited from

Me through My Spirit giving you vitality, new life, and creating My likeness in you. You share My love with those you meet and become My ambassador. You care for My creation and rejoice in Our Spirit union together, forever.

"Now, do you accept or reject My New Covenant? It's a covenant unto death…but that's already been taken care of. There are no negotiations. That's the deal—take it or leave it. What's your decision?"

Hello!

And we listen to the deceiver and buy the lie that it's all just a trick. This must be some kind of manipulation to wreck our fun and keep us from being happy! How could we possibly be happy not controlling every aspect of our lives, protecting our own interests, grabbing whatever we see as good for us, and rejecting or avoiding whatever we think is bad?

It's *The Tree of the Knowledge of Good and Evil* all over again. Only this time, we get to choose. Do we believe God or do we believe the whispers of the accuser? Do we trust God or do we trust ourselves? Do we keep control with self-interest on the throne? Or do we agree to the covenant and let God control the throne of our lives?

We would have to be silly, stubborn idiots not to accept this covenant! Talk about "Let's make a deal!" What a deal!

Okay, so now, what is it we have to do? What is our part in the covenant? Accept the deal ... abdicate the throne ... appreciate the gift ... appropriate what's given.

You see, if we actually realize what has been done on our behalf, we can only stand amazed and grateful. I often hear people pray, "Dear God, help me to have more faith, more love, more trust."

"Well, I have good news!

You don't get any more.

You have all you're going to get

because you have it all!"

We just need to believe it,

use the access we have,

and live in our new identity.
....

God doesn't just have love. *God is love.* God doesn't just have joy. *God is joy.* God doesn't just have peace. *God is peace.* God doesn't just have long-suffering (patience). *He is patience.* God doesn't just have gentleness. *He is gentleness.* God doesn't just have goodness. *He is goodness.* God doesn't just have faithfulness. *He is faithfulness.* God doesn't just possess meekness (unpretentious confidence). *He is meekness.* God doesn't just have temperance (moderation and balance). *He is temperance.*

He says "I am that I am." He is the Great I Am. He is continual *present tense*—with us always. And the most incredible thing for us to understand is that all He is becomes available to us, not because we earn it or deserve it, but because it's *His gift.*

Repeatedly, the scriptures talk about abiding in

Him and Him abiding in us. "Christ *in* you, the hope of glory" (Colossians 1:27, NIV). "I am crucified with Christ: nevertheless I live; yet not I, but Christ liveth in me" (Galatians 2:20).

He promises He will give His Holy Spirit to all who ask. Again, what is the fruit of that Spirit? It's all the things that He is—love, joy, peace, patience, gentleness, goodness, faith, unpretentious confidence, moderation, and balance (Ephesians 5:9).

And if through the New Covenant He gives us all that He is, then who does the gift belong to? *Us! The gift is Him in us*, accepted with no self-interest on our part, no selfishness motivating our hearts. *Being grateful containers* is the only thing we're asked to do. He's the giver. We're the receivers.

Only when self is dethroned will humility be possible. Humility is being totally un-*self*-conscious… and totally *God*-conscious.

> *Humility is not thinking poorly of myself.*
> *It's not thinking of myself at all.*

It's realizing that all I have and all I am is a reflection of my Father, His gift. Nothing to be arrogant about, but rather something to be grateful for.

He is the potter. We are the clay. We are the pots. He is the Treasure. The Treasure goes into the pots. The pot remains the pot and the Treasure remains the Treasure. No matter how long the Treasure is in the pot, the pot will still be the pot. And no matter how long the pot contains the Treasure, the Treasure will still be the Treasure. The pot does not become the Treasure and the Treasure does not become the pot. But, together, there is a union that pours out Treasure to others.

Everything has been done. "It is finished." The New Covenant is in effect for anyone who accepts it. Again, we don't need to pray for more love or more peace or more faith. There is no more. We have it all because we have Him!

If we're not experiencing it, it must be because we've either not agreed to the covenant in the first place, or we're ignoring it. If we don't believe it, don't trust it, and turn off the flow of the Treasure, douse the Lights, self-serve as if no agreement has ever been struck, we won't experience it. Our choice. Do we choose the fruit of self–interest from the *Tree of the Knowledge of Good and Evil*? Or do we choose the fruit of the Spirit from the *Tree of Life*?

Remember the picture of the Old Covenant where they would stand in the middle of the sacrifice and say, with the mixing of the blood, "If I break this covenant, you can cut off my head, cut me in half, and leave me to the birds?" Well, if we agree to the New Covenant and then ignore it, how crazy would that be? Am I saying that God is going to cut us up and leave us to the birds if we break or ignore the covenant? No. *It's exactly the opposite.* Our representative's side was pierced. His flesh was laid open and He was the one hung out for the birds. Just picture Him on the cross.

We can only stand in awe and say…"Thank you!"
All has been done! All is available!
It's pretty silly to be sitting at a feast,
crying and begging for bread.

"The Lord Jesus the same night in which He was betrayed, took bread. And when He had given thanks, He broke it and said, 'Take eat. This is my body which is broken for you. This do in remembrance of me. And this cup is the New Covenant in my blood. This do ye, as oft as ye drink it, in remembrance of me" (1 Corinthians 11:24, 25, author's paraphrase). "He that eateth my flesh, and drinketh my blood, dwelleth in me, and I in Him" (John 6:56).

What an incredible picture! Not one we're used to thinking about in today's world. But in the Old Covenant, remember this? After the sacrifice was made, the sacrifice was eaten. As I've mentioned, that's why God always told them to give their best for the sacrifice.

Well, He gave the best He had for us. And then He said..."Take, eat. See, I have made a feast for you. Take into yourselves everything that I am. Enjoy!"

The picture is plain. The bread and wine symbolize His body and blood. And, regardless of doctrinal variations that may debate the literal or figurative transformation of the elements, the main point remains that of total provision; a continual availability and giving of all that He is to meet our every need.

Science confirms that it's the blood that carries life to every cell. It's the blood that repairs and heals. It's the blood that carries instructions to the rest of the body. He's offering a cleansing transfusion of *His own blood*. In essence, He says, "I'm giving you all that I am. Take all of Me into yourself that you may dwell in Me and I in you. This is my body, the Bread of Life. Take, eat."

Food is what keeps us alive. It nourishes us physically and emotionally. You've heard the phrase, "You are what you eat." Well…how incredible! How wonderful! What an image! And still, some stand begging in the midst of the feast. There is bread and wine in abundance.

The King has come.

The Covenant is made.

Good news! Spread the word. The table is set.

The invitations are sent.

All are welcome at the King's banquet.

So, how do we practically measure our success in all of this? Where are the scales to weigh our efforts? Well, more good news…He is our only success as He lives His life through us. And what effort? There's only choice! And the choice is who we will place on the throne. Is it Self or the King? Trust or Disregard? Belief or Unbelief?

Do you feel His peace regarding an idea or threshold? Then walk ahead confidently. "The steps of a good man are ordered by the Lord" (Psalm 37:23). But, until then and always, we're first and foremost "human beings" not "human doings." His presence has to be internal before it can be external. Faith first, then works. He's given us only one measuring stick and it's this. Do you see the Fruit of the Spirit? "By their fruits you will know them" (Matthew 7:20).

"They will know we are Christians by our love."

That's it! That's all of it!

If we have love, we have Him. If He's abiding in us and us in Him, we'll have love because He *is* love.

It's not something we work at. It's unavoidable. It simply is. It *has* to be.

If we breathe in helium gas, it will make our voice go up high and sound funny. Everyone will know what's inside of us, what we've breathed in, and what we contain. It's not something we work at. It's unavoidable. It simply is. It *has* to be. Likewise, when we're filled with the Zoë breath of God, His Spirit will be evident.

It simply will be.

What good news! The King lives!

The New Covenant has been imposed.

By accepting the covenant, we're proclaimed royalty.

We live under the protection and provision of the New Covenant forever. We're King's kids, enjoying the abiding presence, the radiance, and the loving resemblance of our Father, the King of the Universe.

Now, that's good news!

Something to Think About:

If Christianity is a relationship, not a religion, what part of it involves "good works?"

How would you describe the feeling of having someone else pay your fine or take your punishment?

How would you describe true humility?

What changes would you expect to see in a person's life who'd agreed to the New Covenant? What is God's part of it? What is man's part of it?

CHAPTER FIVE

CONSUMMATING THE DEAL

CHAPTER FIVE

CONSUMMATING THE DEAL

We've talked about how covenants are made and why they came to be. We've talked about the meaning behind covenant. But now I want to share another word picture to help seal the deal in your mind of what the essence of Christianity is.

In living it out, it's experiencing the indwelling "breath of God" by agreeing to the covenant. But how does it actually take place? To understand the relationship being offered by Christ, let's look at the different ways He describes that relationship.

First, we need to understand that Jesus loved everyone. He wasn't a respecter of persons (Acts 10:34). For example, He treated women with dignity and always bolstered their esteem. Wealth, poverty, or social status was inconsequential to Jesus. According to Him, there is no Greek or Jew, no male or female, no superficial standings with God.

In various instances, He likened Himself to being our brother, our friend, our shepherd, and our King. The relationship I want us to think about now, though, is that of bride and groom. Being believers, we're referred to as *His bride*…the "Bride of Christ." That may seem sort of strange. It's a very intimate reference best understood in the context of how marriages took place in Jesus' day.

Here's how it happened. When a marriage was being planned, the groom and his father would go to the bride-to-be and her father's house and they would discuss the price of the bride. (Yeah, you read that right… "the price." It was like the reverse idea of a dowry.) Although it was common for women of that day not to be treated with the same esteem as men … when it came to marriage, a daughter brought a good price. It was usually about the cost of a house.

After the negotiations were complete and a price

was agreed upon, the deal was sealed with *the Cup of Covenant*. This was a glass of wine offered from the groom to his intended. He would extend the glass to his bride and say, "I love you. I *give you* my life. *Will you give me* yours?"

She then had a decision to make. She could either accept his offer and drink the wine or refuse it. If she accepted it, she was saying, "I love you. *I accept* your life and I *give you* mine."

Following the Ceremony of Covenant, the groom and his father would return to their house and the preparations would begin for the wedding. The bride was busy telling all her friends about the event and making herself ready for the celebration and her new home, while the groom was busy building a place to bring his bride home to.

Often, homes of that day were constructed with a courtyard in the center. Then, as each son was married, he would build on to his father's house. This family complex was called an insula. No one could say when the son's place was ready except the father. It was the father who would announce to the son, "Okay. It's ready. Today you can go and get your bride." After all, this was an addition to the father's house. He had to be sure everything was finished in keeping with the rest of his house. So, when that day arrived, the son went to his bride's house and announced, "Today's the day!" She sent out a word to all of her friends and the marriage ceremony, which had long been prepared, took place. Then, the groom escorted his bride back to the place he'd prepared. They would go into their new home and consummate the marriage. Then, they would announce to the best man, "We're married!" The best man would, in turn, announce it to the crowd, and the seven-day party would begin.

Of course, Jesus' first miracle was performed at a wedding. They had run out of wine, which was undoubtedly a great embarrassment to the family. Probably, this was not a very wealthy family and, this time, they simply were not able to get away with *just enough* as they had hoped. But then Jesus stepped in and quietly turned huge jugs of water into wine.

The governor of the feast commented to the bridegroom, "Why have you saved the best wine for last? Most people serve the good wine first" (John 2:10, author's paraphrase).

Our King does not know lack! He isn't a God of *just enough. He's a God of more than enough.* "More than we could ask or think" (Luke 11: 9–13, Matthew 7:7–8). And He comes to each of us and says, *"I love you. I give you my life. Will you give me yours?"* And we have a decision to make. We can refuse to take the extended cup or we can say, "I love you. *I accept* your life, and *I give* you mine." Then He goes on to say, "In my father's house are many mansions (insulas): if it were not so, I would have told you. I go to prepare a place for you ... I will come again, and receive you unto myself; that where I am, there you may be also" (John 14:2).

Do you see the incredible picture here? Do you see why He calls us His bride?

There's another story He tells of the wise virgins and the foolish virgins (Matthew 25). The wise virgins had made preparations for the return of the Groom.

They had oil for their lamps and were waiting for Him to come. The foolish virgins had no oil and were not looking for Him to return. When He arrived, the foolish virgins were surprised and wanted more time to still be able to get ready. They needed to find oil for their lamps. But it was too late.

Biblically speaking, oil is the symbol for the Holy Spirit. Through the covenant, the Groom seals the deal by actually filling us, His lamps, His lights to the world, with His indwelling Spirit, His very presence. However, first, each of us has to answer the Groom's question individually when He says, "I love you. I give you my life. Will you give me yours?"

When He comes back for you, will you be ready? Have you struck the deal? Is there oil in your lamp?

Just tell Him, "I love you, Lord. I accept your life and I give you mine. I give you all of my internal junk to dispose of. Take it away. Thank you for being my scapegoat. Forgive me. Wash me clean. Holy Spirit, I welcome you into the core of my being. Thank you, Lord, for refilling me with all that You are. Blow Your Zoë breath of life into me and let me be clean and new—alive from the inside out. Live in me and let Your light flow through me."

In the name above all names, Jesus. Amen.

Get ready.

He's coming back.

Only the Father knows when.

Something to Think About:

In what way does our relationship with Jesus, being like a marriage, change your thinking about who He is and what His intentions are regarding you?

Do you realize that the "richest" man in the universe has extended His hand to you? What effect should that have? Have you accepted the offer?

ABOUT THE AUTHOR

J. Brooke-Harte

Jan Brooke-Harte is the president and founder of The Foundation Association, a ministry of encouragement and a network of support for pastors and their families, as well as a women's ministry network.

Jan has been featured across the nation as both speaker and singer in such places as The Crystal Cathedral of Garden Grove, California; Fourth Presbyterian Church of Bethesda, Maryland; and Angeles Temple of Los Angeles, California.

As a former college dean of students, youth pastor, and campus life staff, Jan considers herself fortunate to have assisted many students in finding answers to life's most difficult questions.

Variety and versatility describe her life. Her experience ranges from singer/recording artist, actress, marketing/public relations director and entrepreneur, to youth pastor, college dean of students, counselor, and author. She writes children's books, poetry, and apologetics, as well as life stories.

"As the hart panteth after the water brooks, so panteth my soul after thee, O God." Psalm 42:1

REFERENCES

Book of Genesis – Moses

Bock, Darrell L., Johs Chatraw, and Andreas
Kostenberger. *Truth Matters: Confident Faith in
a Confusing World.* Nashville: B&H Academic,
2014.

DeHann, Mart and Jimmy DeYoung. *Day of
Discovery: Israel Series.*

Dobson, James and Ray VanderLaan. "That the
World May Know." https://www.thatthe-
worldmayknow.com/.

Gospel of John – The Apostle John

Ham, Ken. "The Institute for Creation
Research." https://www.icr.org/research.

Lewis, C.S. *Mere Christianity.* United Kingdom: Geoffrey Bles, 1952.

Ravi Zacharias Ministries. "Ask?"

Smith, Malcolm. *Spiritual Burnout.* Colorado Springs: Honor Books, 1977.

Sproul, R.C. *The Glory of Christ.* Phillipsburh, NJ: P & R Publishing, 2003.

Strobel, Lee. *The Case for Christ:Investigating the Evidence of Belief.* Grand Rapids: Zondervan, 2009.